This is dedicated to my wife Sharon, my

Sharon, the most wonderful woman in t
beyond.

CW01395070

Mum, the bravest and most amazing wo......,
than just my mum, my inspiration, my best friend, I love you.

Ian, who fought so bravely against cancer and sadly lost his battle, I will always
cherish the many happy memories I have, and you will forever be in my heart.

To Chris
with best wishes
love from
Nic +

FOREWORD

Being dyslexic and having OCD, it really wasn't easy for me to write a book. I am a perfectionist and I am my own worst critic.

Someone once asked me, what do you want to do in life, what do you really want to be?

I thought about this long and hard and wasn't really sure for quite a while, but my passion lays in writing poetry about the experiences I've had, the places I've been, the friends I've made and the things and people I love the most.

My favourite poet once said, "I've learned that people will forget what you say, people will forget what you did, but people will never forget how you made them feel".

This is so true, all the poems I have written in my book are all true feelings and emotions of what I have been through or seen on my journey in life so far. Some of the poems are long, some are short, some are funny, and some will make you cry, but they are all true.

The pain, the joy, the sadness, the love and the many smiles of happiness are what I write about. Thoughts just come into my head and I just have to write them down (whatever time it may be) and keep going until a poem appears. I am not the most intelligent person and I may not be very academic but everything I write is written from the heart, it is genuine and is written with such honesty and truth.

I have always loved reading poetry, but it was meeting my wife Sharon that made me realise how much I love poetry and found out I could write it as well. To me she is the most wonderful woman in the world, she inspires me so much, she never puts me down, she believes in me and wants me to be the best I can be. As you will see while reading this book I have the deepest love for her and it's thanks to her that I started writing poetry. She makes my life complete and has made me the happiest person in the world. I am so proud of her and the day I married my wife and took her name was the best day of my life. I feel very privileged and honoured that she has let me put some of her own poetry at the end of my book for you all to enjoy too.

WRITTEN BY NICOLA DE-FREITAS

CONTENTS:

35. My Love For You

36. Mum's Mother's Day Poem

37. Dad's Father's Day Poem

38. Beautiful Pillows

39. Drip

40. Happy Choccy Day

41. Tattoo For AJ

42. Uncle Tony

43. Deep Blue

44. Pixie

45. What A Wonderful World

46. Beautiful Little Birdies

47. Moving

48. Pastures New

49. Honey Bunny

50. I Love You More

51. Just Wanted To Say .....

52. You Know

53. Cheer Up Sunshine

54. Living The Dream

55. Sheryl's Birthday Poem

56. Little One

57. My Mum In Law

58. Kevin

59. Aga

60. A Better Place

61. Wedding Vows Happy Ever After

62. Please Get Better Soon

63. Everyone's In Pain But Love Conquers All

64. Treasure Is The Meaning Of Love

65. Not Intelligent But No Less Of A Person

66. Lyn And Lou

67. Debbie

68. Crohn's Disease

69. Wendy

70. Theatre

71. Alzheimer's

72. For The Love Of Kittens

73. My Wedding Day

74. Cancer

75. Marco

SHARON DE-FREITAS

Sweetheart,

Heavenly,

Amazing,

Radiant,

Outstanding,

Nurture,

Desirable

Enlighten,

Fantastic,

Romantic,

Enchanting,

Impressive,

Thoughtful,

Attraction,

Spectacular.

SHARON DE-FREITAS XX

Sweetheart is what you are to me,

Holding you in my arms I would love to be,

Anywhere in the world with you I would go,

Riding all over and enjoying the view,

Our lives being shared with us hand in hand,

Now walking together along the sea in the sand,

Destined to be together I'm sure we are,

Everlasting love is what we have by far,

Forever there and just loving each other,

Raining sometimes but we head for cover,

Ever there for each other even when we are blue,

Inspire me is what you always do,

This is the best feeling in the world,

And forever I want to be in your hold,

Someone I treasure, I just want to be near,

XX Kissing and cuddling I wish you were here.

I LOVE YOU SO

I Love you so oh yes, I do,

Love like this is special too,

Over the moon and as happy as can be,

Very wonderful beautiful woman I see,

Even when you're not in my arms,

You always make me feel safe and calm,

Our love is just meant to be,

Underneath the stars and so happy,

So, no need to ever feel blue,

Oh, I love you yes, I do.

FOREVER YOURS

Feelings like this have never been so strong,

Our love for each other could never be wrong,

Right here with me is where you'll be,

Everlasting love I know you can see,

Very happy is what we are,

Eternity with you we will go far,

Romance and love fill our hearts,

You know I love you right from the start,

Our hopes and dreams are all coming true,

Under the sun with the sky so blue,

Right now, our lives together and long,

Smiles so wide and our beautiful song.

HOW I SEE MYSELF

Acceptance……………….is always what I want,

Better……………………………………………….I need to be,

O.K…………………………….never bad and never good,

Unconfident………………………………….that's just me,

Try…………………………………………..is what I always do,

Matter……………………………………………….do I?

Yearning……………………………………..to be loved,

Self Esteem………………………..I don't have much,

Encouragement………………………..is what I need,

Large…………………………that's me, its who I am,

Forgive…………………………………myself, I need to do.

ABOUT ME

I love the colour blue,

I love the popstar Pink.

I love to help and do,

I love to have a think.

I love to have a laugh,

I love to make and cook,

I love a bubble bath,

I love to read a book.

I love to see the smiles,

I love to live my life,

I love to walk for miles,

I'd love to have a wife.

I love the birds and bees,

I love to hear them sing,

I love the flowers and the tree's,

I love most everything.

I love my friends and family,

I love to play my darts,

I love to live in harmony,

I love to feel people's hearts.

JACK

When you were born, you were so small,

And now you're growing and becoming tall,

You have beautiful blue eyes and golden hair,

And a smile so wonderful I see it there.

Your hands they are the same as ours,

We would cuddle up with you for hours,

Learning to walk and then to run,

Seeing you laugh and having fun.

You would go off swimming in the pool,

And now you've even started school,

You are now growing up to be a big boy,

But you will always be my bundle of joy.

LIZ

Her name was Liz she was my mate,

We had lots of fun and it was great,

We both used to play darts,

We'd have such a good laugh.

Off out clubbing is where we'd go,

Drinking breezer's and dancing the night through,

She was so beautiful, and all heads would turn,

Her favourite flower Lilly's is what she would yearn.

We spent lots of time together until,

She was poorly and became ill,

I saw her there in so much pain,

It made me cry, I wanted someone to blame.

She was so brave, and she never complained,

Then a bright light from heaven came,

She was so wonderful and so smart,

She will always be forever in my heart.

SCHOOL

I was never any good at school,

I was made to feel like such a fool,

Even though I'd go the extra yard,

I always found everything so hard.

Whenever we had an exam or test,

Everything always seemed to go west,

You're not trying is what they'd say,

But I tried so hard I never had time to play.

I never said much, I was a little shy,

I had no confidence, I don't know why,

I didn't mess around like all the rest,

I tried so hard to do my best.

As a person, I'm not so bad,

But at school I felt so sad,

I don't know why they couldn't see,

Deep within 'THE REAL ME'.

MARKET SQUARE

My family used to work on Northampton Market Square,

We had a greengrocer's stall that we stood upon there,

Three generations of my family worked on it for 57 years,

Serving lots of people from the young to the old dears.

We always had our regulars that would come every week,

We used to stand in all weathers even when it was bleak,

We had fresh fruit and vegetables we sold every day,

People used to come for them from far far away.

We all worked very hard it was not an easy job to do,

We used to lift heavy boxes and sacks of spuds the whole day through,

We all started very early at half past six in the morning,

When everybody else were not up yet and hadn't started yawning.

With all the other traders, we used to get on very well,

There are many funny stories I recall of that we could tell,

We were like a family and always there for each other,

Helping anyone out if there was any kind of bother.

There were many happy years that my family and I had,

Lots of fun and many happy memories, it really wasn't bad,

57 years we worked on their it didn't seem to feel so long,

I miss it from time to time now that it has gone.

MY SHINING STAR

There she is my little shining star,

Now she's in my life I know we're gonna go far,

Makes me so happy I feel like I could fly,

Before I met her all I did was cry,

Now the tears have all gone away,

And love fills my heart and I want it to stay,

She sees me for the person I am,

And loves me just because she can,

She sees all the good things in me,

And wants me to be the best I can be,

She understands me and feels the same,

And no more do I feel like I'm going insane,

Now my life feels like it has just begun,

I'm so lucky now I know I've found the one,

She's the best in the world and I never want to be apart,

Because I love her from the bottom to the top of my heart,

Beautiful, smart, wonderful and funny is what you are,

Sharon, you will always be my little shining star.

ALWAYS

Have no fear, I'll always be here,

Please be aware, I will always care,

If you are feeling ill, then I'll get you a pill,

Anything I would do, I'll take care of you,

If you are sad, or feeling bad,

I'll make you laugh, and run you a bath,

If you have a bad day, to me you can say,

We can go for a walk, if you ever need to talk,

If you are ever in lumber, you have my number,

Give me a dial, and I'll give you a smile,

If we ever argue, I'll always forgive you,

Never be sorry, you don't have to worry,

I'll always be free, if you ever need me,

I'll hold you in my arms, and keep you safe from harm,

If you ever need to cry, on me you can rely,

I am the one, you can depend upon,

I'll give you pleasure, for you I do treasure,

You are my life, maybe one day my wife,

I'll be there for you, there's nothing I wouldn't do,

I'll stop you falling apart, because I have hold of your heart.

EVERYTHING ABOUT YOU I LOVE

I love to stare into your eyes,

Because they just mesmerise.

I love to just hold your hand,

No matter where we might stand.

I love to hold you in my arms,

Where I can keep you safe from harm.

I love to run my fingers through your hair,

And always do this with so much care.

I love to watch you in the tub,

And then give you a foot rub.

I love to give you a back massage,

It always makes your smile go large.

I love to lay my head upon your chest,

This feeling is just the best.

I love it when we kiss,

There's no other feeling like this.

I love to feel your skin touch mine,

This feeling is just divine.

I like to suck on your finger,

It makes me feel like I want to linger.

I love to feel your inner thighs,

So I can hear all your sighs.

I love to feel your so hard nipples,

I like to go around with my tongue like ripples.

I love it when our tongues do dance,

It puts me into a trance.

I love to feel you where I tingle,

My heart feels like it's in a tangle.

I love to feel you deep inside,

It makes my heartbeat just go wild.

I love it when we both make love,

It makes me feel I'm in heaven above.

I love it when we come together,

It makes me feel as light as a feather.

I want to lick and suck your taste,

There is no drop that I want to waste.

I love to stroke your beautiful face,

It makes my heart speed up its pace.

I love to squeeze your lovely bum,

The feeling is just so yum.

Even before the day we met,

You've always made me feel so wet.

I love to see your beautiful smile,

I just can't stop there's no denial.

I love to watch you when you sleep,

All my love for you to keep.

I love to listen to you breathe

I never ever want you to leave.

I love it when you are being funny,

It makes the day feel so sunny.

I love to hear you when you giggle,

And see the way it makes you wiggle.

I love your taste you have in music,

And the way you like to share it.

I love the way you are competitive,

And the way you are not negative.

I love the way you are so clever,

Stop amazing me, no you could never.

I love the way you have faith in me,

And all the good that you do see.

I love the way your words just flow,

When you write about your woe.

I love the poems that you write,

With such wonder and delight.

You are so good in everything that you do,

And the way you are is always true.

The things you say with thought and meaning,

Always leave me completely beaming.

I love to be with you all the time,

I love to know that you are just mine.

In and out, top to bottom you are so beautiful,

I was telling the truth when I say you are so wonderful!

LOVE NEVER DIES

There are people in my life, that I have loved and lost
They all mean a lot to me, much more than any cost.
I remember them all the time which always leaves me beaming,
The fondest of memories to treasure with such warm feeling.

There was my pap, Sam Lemon, a most wonderful man liked by many.
There was my nan, Grace Lemon, who was always there for me.
There was Liz, my amazing friend, with whom I had such fun.
There was the little one, I haven't had the pleasure to meet yet.
There was my pap, Peter Savage, a very popular and much-loved man.
There was my nan, Doris Savage, who could always make me laugh.

I would love to hold you all in my arms again and give you all a kiss.
It's a privilege and an honour to know you and all of you I do miss.
Each and every one will forever have a special place in my heart,
I will see you all again in heaven when it is my time to depart.

BETTY AND GEORGE

I love to watch you both dance,

You look as if you're in a trance.

To see you both look into each other's eyes,

It's wonderful to see that love is still alive.

Both in each other's arms as you glide across the floor,

Just makes everyone want to watch you more and more.

Listening to the music and hearing it rhyme,

Both of you stepping together, moving in time.

Step by step, like the beating of a heart,

Dancing together and never wanting to be apart.

You dance so beautiful together and it's so nice to see,

That love lasts forever, the way it's meant to be.

SEVEN DAYS APART

Far away is where I might be.

In my arms, I wish you were

Right here tenderly kissing me.

Standing next to me right here,

Together forever one day we will be.

Still missing you,

Even more than before.

Can't wait to hold you,

Only want you more.

Never want to leave you,

Dearest love, I do adore.

This is where I want to be with you.

Here with us both enjoying the view,

In each other's arms, holding tightly too.

Right now, the sun is shining, and the sky is so blue.

Dreams are real and can all come true.

First times, so many more to come.

Over time we'll make our home,

Using each day to love each other more,

Romance and love we both adore.

This is the life for me,

Here with my wife to be.

For me you are meant to be,

In my arms, I love to see.

For my heart, you have the key,

Together we'll be drinking tea.

Having you forever with me.

Sexy is all of you,

Incredible that's just you

X X X X kisses all for you

Thinking all the time of you

Here I am all for you.

Special is my wonderful woman,

Everlasting love, you are the one

Value you, you're the one in a million

Exquisite is just you baby

No one else, you are my lady

There is no one else in the world

Having you there just to hold.

PRINCESS ALEX

Playing darts is such good fun,

Round the board to number one.

In the league, the first division,

Not losing many competitions.

Come every week to try our best,

Endless times we beat the rest.

Super bunch of girls we have,

Splendid times that we have had.

All the pubs that we go to

Laughing always gets us through.

Every game that we play

eXciting times all the way.

ADRIAN AND HANAN

Teenage sweethearts you were, now been together for years,

Made for each other and meant to be, it appears.

Your beautiful wedding day on the beach in Thailand,

Both of you there by the sea with you hand in hand.

Your second wedding day in England right here,

All your family members and friends were there.

Now you are both as happy as can be,

At the beginning of making your own family.

All your hopes and dreams are now coming true,

Many happy memories are wished for both of you.

Now husband and wife building a life together,

May you have many happy years together forever.

RICHARD, MY LITTLE BRO'

I'm so lucky I have such a fab little brother,

He's the best brother ever, there is no other.

Everything he does is always does to his best,

A heart so big that he has in his chest.

He's a grown man now, but my little bro' he will always be,

He is a wonderful person and he means the world to me.

He's so good at his job and he works so very hard,

He does everything he can to go the extra yard.

He plays bowls for county and he's had an England trial,

Not picked this time, but he will be in a while.

He's an amazing Dad to Jack and he loves him so,

He takes him out everywhere, all over they go.

I'm so proud of him and everything he does,

He's the best brother in the world and will forever have my love.

MY PARENTS

My Mum and Dad they are the best,

They are better than all the rest.

They are both so proud of me,

It's down to them I am the person you see.

Whenever I am down and feeling a bit sad,

They're always there to stop me feeling bad.

They care about me and we have a laugh,

There are many happy memories that we do have.

I'm not quite the person they thought I would be,

But I am who I am, and they still love me.

They are liked by all and have many friends,

The people's love for them just never ends.

They're the best parents that could ever be,

They are so wonderful and amazing to me.

I really want them both to know,

That I really do love them so.

LYN

You were my first love, but now you are my friend,

We've been through a lot together and on each other we did depend.

You were always there for me getting me through any kind of woe,

Without your love and support, how I would have got through, I really do not know.

We laughed a lot and many happy times is what we had,

Six and a half wonderful years together it really wasn't bad.

We are not together, as a couple we are no more,

But my life, you made it so much happier than before.

We were not right for each other and it wasn't meant to be,

But I don't regret a single minute as you mean a lot to me.

I know that I was not the right person for you,

But I hope that I made you happy while we were together too.

For the future years to come I give to you my very best wishes,

And I hope all good things come to you and find you happiness.

If you ever need a mate on me you can depend,

You've always meant a lot to me and I will forever be your friend.

HOLIDAYS

Happy times with mates to be made in the sun,

Our laughter so loud with us all having fun.

Loving to swim and dip in the pool,

In we jump to the clear water so cool.

Dancing and singing the night away,

Always having a good time as we play.

Yes, relaxing and chilling we definitely can,

Sunbathing and getting a tan is the plan.

YOU ARE.....

You are the air which keeps me alive,

You are the taste that's nectar to me,

You are the beauty I see with my eyes,

You are the caring soul that I see.

You are the scent so sweet and sensational,

You are the touch I always have a longing for,

You are the happiness which makes me smile,

You are the need inside me I want more and more.

You are the thoughts that are constantly in my mind,

You are the love that fills my heart,

You are the missing piece I was searching for to find,

You are the one, now my life can start.

MISSING YOU

I miss you when I wake up and you're not there,

My bed feels very cold and very bare.

I want to see your beautiful eyes and stare,

And I want to run my fingers through your hair.

To lay my head on your chest, what a wonderful pair,

To see your amazing smile as bright as a flare.

I want to kiss you all over your body everywhere,

And make love to you as many times as we dare.

When you're not there it's like waking up from a nightmare,

Because you are my world and for you I REALLY DO CARE.

CHRISTMAS WITH YOU…..

Christmas time should always be fun,

Spending time with your loved one.

I wish I was there to give you a kiss,

To see your beautiful smile would be bliss.

All the gifts sitting under the tree,

There with you is where I would love to be.

I'd love to watch you open your presents,

And see all the gifts that you've been sent.

To be snuggled up together by the fire,

After we had enjoyed our Christmas dinner.

We'd watch Christmas films together on TV,

Then a bath with you is where I'd love to be.

A loving kiss under the mistletoe,

Off to bed for a cuddle we would go.

Coffee with Bailey's to keep us warm,

We wouldn't have to set an alarm.

Making love to each other we would be,

So wonderful, I love you and you love me.

CHRISTMAS WISHES

Christmas time is very near,

Santa Claus will soon be here.

The shopping is now all done,

And there are presents for everyone.

The tree is up and it's looking good,

The foods all ready and we've made a pud.

Family and friends to meet and see,

And lots of cheer there will surely be.

A wonderful Christmas for everyone,

With lots of laughter and much fun.

The stars are all shining brightly above,

Best wishes are sent with lots of love.

I LOVE SHARON

I love Sharon De-Freitas

And she loves me,

I have never been so happy

I glow with glee.

She is my world

And I hers too,

Whenever she's around

I never feel blue.

She is amazing

And she is my life,

She loves me so much

And wants me to be her wife.

I love her with all my heart

I always want us to be together,

In love with each other

For always and forever.

SWEET PEA

Sharon is my sexy little Sweet pea,

Whenever I am with her she always makes me happy.

Even when we are apart she brings a smile to my face,

Every time I think of her my heart picks up its pace.

The saying is that the best things in life are free,

Priceless is my sweet pea and the only one for me.

Every day is wonderful, and everything feels new,

Adore and love her always, my whole life through and through.

PROJECTS 'THE A TEAM'

It will soon be time for me to be going on my way,

But don't be sad because I know I'm gonna be ok.

My time spent here with both of you has been a happy time,

It has been an absolute pleasure and it's also been sublime.

I will miss you both a lot, of this I am very sure,

But just because I'm not here does not mean we're not mates anymore.

I hope we'll all keep in touch and remember the happy times we've had,

This is now a new start for me so please don't look so sad.

It's a cheerio for now but not a definite goodbye,

I won't be gone forever, I will tell you both for why.

We'll both be back very soon for our wedding day,

Of which you're both invited to of course I have to say.

The years I'm gone might be two or three or maybe seven or eight,

But we'll both definitely be back even though I do not know the date.

I class you both as my friends and you mean a lot to me,

I'll never forget you because in my heart you both will always be.

PRINCESS ALEX DARTS TEAM

It will soon be time for me to go because I must depart,

But don't be sad, because for me, this is a brand-new start.

I will miss you all terribly, of this I can't deny,

But it's just a farewell for now, not a definite goodbye.

Although I will not be here, my company you will lack,

I will only be gone for a while, because one day I will be back.

Please don't ever forget me, and the happy times we've had,

We've been through so much together, all the happy and the sad.

You've no idea how much happiness you all have given to me,

I will not be without you, close my eyes and there you'll be.

On Thursdays for a while I will not be here to throw a dart,

But I will always be part of the team, as you'll always be in my heart.

TO MY VALENTINE

I've never felt love like this before,

I can't help but love you more and more.

All day long I'm thinking of you,

And all the lovely things we'll do.

All the places we can go and see,

And all the first times that there will be.

All the special moments that we will share,

The tough times together we'll both bare.

The fun and laughs we'll have together,

I know that this will last forever.

I love you and you love me,

Together as one we will be.

SNOW

When I was little I liked the snow,

Now I'm older I wish it would go.

It was great to have a snowball fight,

Now I worry if I'll get home alright.

Building a snowman was such good fun,

Now I just hope I don't slip over on my bum.

I'd dream of ice skating on a frozen lake,

Now I'm scared of all the bones I could break.

When I was little I liked the snow,

Now I'm older I wish it would go.

CAKES

There is so much that I could make,

Lots of cakes that I can bake.

I like to do lots of different things,

Now I'm getting out my baking tins.

Making a cake that tastes of chocolate,

Then decorating them, looks so delicate.

Lots of different muffins to do,

All the colours from yellow to blue.

Rolling and cutting out lots of scones,

Currants and raisins in hot cross buns.

Homemade suet or steamed fruit pud,

With custard always tastes so good.

It's always good to lick out the bowl,

When you're making a lovely swiss roll.

Different jams and buttercreams,

They all just taste like a dream.

Topped with piped flowers or maybe cherries,

Chocolate buttons or sweets or berries.

Any type at all to make is always fun,

And they look so pretty, and they taste really yum.

HARDER GOODBYE'S

It gets harder each time we have to say goodbye,

I never want to leave you, of this I can't deny.

Not to be able to see your beautiful smile,

Always makes me sad for a little while.

Not seeing you each day, I really do hate,

But then we arrange our new meeting date.

I know then I will see you very soon,

And this makes me feel over the moon.

Every day until then you I do miss,

Every day I give your picture a kiss.

To see you again I want this very much,

Every fibre in my body is longing for your touch.

MY LOVE FOR YOU

You are the light of my life, my beautiful little sweet pea flower,

The love we share for each other has magnitudes of power.

I love you more than anything that there is in the world,

I will be here for you forever to have you and to hold.

All the time there is in the world would never be enough for me,

Into the next life, to infinity and beyond, loving you for eternity I will be.

The sun shines so brightly in the beautiful sky so baby blue,

I've never seen such a wonderful smile that's on the gorgeous face of you.

The care, the love, the devotion, the happiness and the laughter,

Is in us both as we are one and now are living happily ever after.

I can't believe how lucky I am to have such a wonderful woman in my life,

I feel very proud and very honoured that one day you will be my wife.

There is nothing ever in the world that I would not do for you,

For you are my life, my everything and I will always love you true.

I will always be your lover, even after our atoms have dispersed,

We'll be pushing up daises and my crush will just be getting worse,

And I will follow you into the next life like a dog chasing after a hearse.

MUMS MOTHERS DAY POEM

My mums the best, she's number one,

We always have such good fun.

Sometimes we'll go out shopping together,

Or have a coffee and a bit of a natter.

I can talk to her about anything at all,

She's always there to help, whatever time I call.

The old jokes she tells can still make me laugh,

Every Thursday night we go out and play darts.

We both play bingo and always share when we win,

We go out for a meal to the local Indian.

Sometimes we have each other round for dinner,

We can both cook, and the food just tastes yummier.

When I'm short she's always there to lend me money,

We car boot together when the weather is sunny.

There are numerous jobs we have worked together in,

A great time together we have when we're working.

The dinner and dance we both have a boogie,

And we both cry when we watch a sad movie.

I take after her, neither one of us can sing,

But no one's perfect, can't be good at everything.

She's not just my mum, she is also my best friend,

The most amazing mum there is in the world.

She is so wonderful and very special to me,

And I will always love her for all eternity.

DADS FATHERS DAY POEM,

I love my dad because he's the best,

He's better than everyone, all the rest.

He has always been right there for me,

The best dad in the world he will always be.

I remember the times that he'd walk me to school,

My hand in his, in his glove when it was cold.

At the gate he'd be there waiting for me to meet,

Sometimes I was lucky, and he'd buy me some sweets.

Now I'm older he'd rather buy me a pint,

Meet up in a pub occasionally at night.

Sometimes we go on the bowls tour together,

We have lots of fun and there's always much laughter.

I'm not a little girl anymore, now grown into a woman,

Now I begin a new life with my girlfriend Sharon.

My dad will be there to give me away on my wedding day,

But daddy's little girl to him I will always stay.

He's so amazing, clever and wonderful to me,

Love him forever, the best dad in the world he will always be.

BEAUTIFUL PILLOWS

I love your beautiful pillows, they're the best in the world,

I love to touch them and have them in my hold.

To have my face between them is the best place to be,

To have them in my mouth is absolute bliss to me.

I love to lay beside you and put my head upon your chest,

Or push them both together and in my mouth is the best.

Hold them in my hands and let my tongue have a lick,

Round and round your nipples and then up and down I flick.

My palm around your nipples to stop them getting cold,

I love your beautiful pillows, they're the best in the world.

DRIP

Drip, drip, drip goes my nose,

It's running just like a hose.

I don't like having a cold in my head,

All it does is make me want to stay in bed.

My nose and throat feel like they are on fire,

And going to work really has no desire.

Taking tablets with a lemon drink and honey,

Tissues all around me from my nose that is so runny.

Coughing and sneezing the whole day through,

I hope it's just a cold, and I havn't got the flu.

HAPPY CHOCCY DAY

I hope you have a happy day

Now Easter time is here,

With lots of chocolate all the way

To last you through the year.

An egg, a chick or a little bunny

Galaxy, Wispa, Flake or Kit Kat,

Whatever you get it will be yummy

In plain, milk or white chocolate.

TATTOO FOR AJ

To draw is what you like to do,

And pretty good you are too!

There's lots of people to draw pictures for,

They're queuing right out of the door!

On demand your designs for a tattoo,

Out of everyone they always say Oooohhhh!

UNCLE TONY

My Uncle Tony likes to have a nice cup of tea,

When he goes for a walk on holiday by the sea.

To sit on the front in a café and read the paper,

Then visiting a museum before playing bowls later.

He likes to do crosswords or play a game of chess,

But listening to classical music I thinks he likes best.

Breath in the fresh air while taking in the view,

And visiting different pubs for a real ale or two.

He likes to read books and he likes poetry too,

I've written some poems which he likes to read through,

Do the pub quiz over a pint with his brother,

He is my Uncle Tony and I will love him forever.

DEEP BLUE

The sea is so beautiful with the colour so blue,

With miles and miles of a wonderful view.

It's so very large and the waters so deep,

With amazing dolphins, out of the water they leap.

All different creatures, all great and small,

Beautiful colours and shapes for them all.

Small and large fish all swimming about,

And dangerous sharks, you'd better watch out!

Long silver eels and orange and white clown fish,

Cod and tuna that would make a tasty dish.

Blue and yellow fish and little sea horses,

Pretty coloured corals with prickly anemone's.

Jelly fish can give a very nasty sting,

And very huge whales that like to sing.

Seagulls above trying to catch some dinner,

Seals and sea lions are a wonderful swimmer.

So many beautiful creatures in the deep blue sea,

What a wonderful view for the eyes to see.

PIXIE

I had a little Javan sparrow
And his name was Pixie,
He used to sit behind his mirror
And play beep po with me.

He loved to do a little dance
He used to jump up and down,
Eat millet all day given half the chance
With him about I never had a frown.

He would bath at least once a day
He used to sing a little song,
But not a word that he would say
In all his eight years long.

Splashing about in the bath
He would always get me wet,
All the little chats we'd have
Look at me and tilt his head.

He used to whistle a little tune

And I would whistle back,

I loved him all the way to the moon

And his company now I do lack.

As one day when I awoke

He did not answer me,

And then my little heart it broke

Up in heaven my Pixie now will be.

WHAT A WONDERFUL WORLD

I love animals, wildlife and nature
They're such a wonderful thing,
All the different birds we have
And all the ways they sing.

The trees and fields all so green
The clouds in the sky so blue,
The waves all splashing in the sea
What a beautiful, wonderful view.

Gorgeous flowers in different colours
Some of them with amazing scents,
Bugs and birds and animals
All running around in wonderment.

The snow is cold but looks so pretty
The sun in the sky will shine,
The rain it hydrates everything
The wind in your hair feels divine.

Fields all full of strawberries

And trees with apples so sweet,

Bushes all full up with beans

And potatoes in fields of peat.

Little streams that flow to rivers

Rivers that run to the sea,

If it wasn't for the humans that destroy it

What a wonderful world this could be.

BEAUTIFUL LITTLE BIRDIES

I love birds, they are beautiful
Flying way up high in the sky,
Little tiny ones and bigger ones
Fluttering as they go by.

Little blue and yellow coloured Blue Tits
Flapping their tiny little wings,
Sitting in the branches of an old oak tree
Sounding so beautiful as she sings.

I love the black and white Wagtail
His lovely tail is quite long,
So graciously he glides as he flies
Down on the ground he jumps along.

Pretty coloured little Goldfinches
Gently pecking on the bird seed,
Sitting on the wooden perches
As frantically they do feed.

Wonderful brown coloured Sparrows

All lining up on the wall,

Taking it in turns to eat

Chirping to each other they call.

A beautiful pair of Blackbirds

Male with a bright yellow beak,

Nesting high up in the tree

Trying to find worms to eat.

Then a great big Wood Pigeon

Flicking as he eats his food,

Head nodding up and down as he walks

Making lots of noise as he coos.

A noisy group of Starlings

Pushing each other out of the way,

Fighting over all the food

And squawking all day as they play.

All different kinds of pretty birds

Even a wonderful Dove,

They're all such beautiful creatures

And all of them I love.

MOVING

Boxes and boxes everywhere

Some over here and some over there,

Boxes full of cuddly toys, keyrings, DVD's

Board games, jewellery boxes, books and CD's.

Will it all fit? I just don't know

I'm really, really hoping so,

With suitcases full of all my clothes

A box full of all my slippers and shoes.

All these boxes and bags to lift

Because all my stuff I have to shift,

Then when I'm gone, and I arrive in London

All these bags and boxes have to be undone.

PASTURES NEW

All of my family and friends I will miss,

Before I go I'll give them a cuddle and a kiss,

My home, my job, my town I have to leave,

But a better life for me, I will now have I believe,

Lots of people I have to say goodbye,

But new friends I will make, even though I am shy,

I now have a family all of my own,

My life it has changed, and I have now grown,

I'm a little bit scared of all the changes I make,

But I will soon settle in with Sharon, my wife to take,

I hope it doesn't take long to find me a job,

Because I can't stay at home, I am not a lazy slob,

My first part time job I had when I was nine,

School, college and work has kept me busy all the time,

Everything I have, I have always worked hard for,

If something I could not afford, I would work more and more,

Save up all my money, I just had to wait,

Everything I have I look after and appreciate,

I need a job soon, and hope I find one quickly,

For now, I need to look after and provide for my own family,

Although this is a big change and new for me,

I know I will be happy, living my dream I will be.

HONEY BUNNY

I had a rabbit years ago and her name was Honey,

And she was an Angora long haired bunny,

I used to sit with her for hours and stroke her on her head,

I talked to her a lot of the time and she listened to what I said,

She had one ear up and one ear to the side,

She was so beautiful, and she filled my heart with pride.

She looked so big with all her hair,

But underneath there was hardly anything there,

When there was a storm she used to get a bit scared,

She stamped her foot when the lightening appeared,

I would take her to my room where I'd give her a cuddle,

Thunder and lightening outside but inside we would huddle.

She'd give me a kiss every day to get a chocolate drop,

We spent a lot of time together and we loved each other a lot,

Occasionally I would give her some toast but dandelion leaves she loved best,

Even more than cabbage leaves, sprouting broccoli and all the rest,

She was over eight years old when she passed away and went to sleep,

I loved her so and always will, I have lots of good memories to keep.

I LOVE YOU MORE

I love you more than you could ever know,

I love you more than the highest tree could grow,

I love you more than every single flower ever to be sent,

I love you more than every single little present.

I love you more than all the stars up in the sky,

I love you more than the mountains all so high,

I love you more than every single person there ever was,

I love you more with all my heart and the love it has.

I love you more and more each single day,

I love you more than any words could ever say,

I love you more than you could ever be told,

I love you more than anything in the world.

JUST WANTED TO SAY

Just thought that I would say hello

Because I hate it when I have to go,

Soon I will be there again

Everything will be alright then.

I think about you every day

One day closer is what we say,

Soon I will have my arms wrapped around you

And kissing and cuddling is what we can do.

I don't know what I'd do without you there

My life would be awful, my life would be bare,

When I saw you, in love I did fall

My love for you is the greatest love of all.

I will always love you just a little bit more

More than anyone has been loved before,

You are my beautiful, wonderful little sweet pea

You are the most perfect woman for me.

YOU KNOW

You know how much I love you so,

You know that I would never let you go,

You know you mean the world to me,

You know with you always happy I will be,

You know you are my life, my everything,

You know for you I would do anything,

You know you are wonderful and gorgeous,

You know with you I am amorous,

I really hope that you do know,

You know how much I LOVE YOU SO.

CHEER UP SUNSHINE

Don't look so sad,

It's not all bad,

Just try to be happy,

And become more chatty,

You look a bit down,

But don't wear a frown,

It seems things aren't going your way,

But tomorrow is another day,

If things are feeling a little bit low,

There's only one way they can go,

The sad feeling will go away,

And everything will be ok,

Things will get better, you'll see in time,

So, come on smile, cheer up sunshine.

LIVING THE DREAM

Love waking up and seeing you lay there next to me,

It feels so wonderful and is the best place to be,

Very fast my heart beats as I watch you as you breath,

I then wonder what it is about that you dream.

Now I hear the little sparrows as they happily sing away,

Grow a smile on my face while next to you I lay,

The most wonderful woman in the world is all mine,

Holding you and touching you always feels divine.

Every time I look at you I see how beautiful you are,

Do anything for you with all my love and my care,

Right here next to you is where I'll be as long as I live,

Everything I am and have is what to you I give.

All the special moments and the memories we make,

May we both cherish them forever with our love no one can break.

SHERYL'S BIRTHDAY POEM

If we were millionaires

We would treat you to,

A choccywoccydoda cake

Made especially for you.

Shape it like a vodka bottle

With an apple on the label,

You could eat it by the slice

Or maybe by the ladle.

Fill it full of apple jam

And lots and lots of cream,

Make it taste so wonderful

It's always in your dreams.

We don't have any money left

The bank account has had it,

So, all you got was this card

The front has a fridge magnet.

LITTLE ONE

Welcome to the world my dear
It's been nine months now you are here,
Your beauty now for all to see
Mum and Dad, they are so happy.

Your little fingers and your toes
Your gorgeous eyes and your button nose,
The smile upon your little face
The beat of your heart with such a pace.

So much for you to learn and see
Many happy times there will be,
So many things to experience and do
A lot of laughs your whole life through.

Your life now has just begun
I hope you have a lot of fun,
The very best is wished for you
In everything that you may do.

MY MUM IN LAW

I call her mum,

I care for her like my mum,

I love her like my mum,

I hold her arm when we walk,

I take her hand when getting off a bus,

I help her dress if she needs me to,

I look after her when she's sick,

I go to the doctors with her,

I take her to hospital appointments,

I'm there for her when she wobbles,

I'm ready to catch her when she falls,

When I get home from work the first

Thing I do is check mum is ok,

The first thing she does is ask me

How my day went,

We talk together,

I listen to all her stories, (again and again),

And all of her little sayings,

We laugh together,

We shop together,

We are there for each other,

She is exactly like my mum,

She's so funny, I'm proud of her,

She's wonderful, she's amazing,

She is my friend,

I call her mum,

I care for her like my mum,

I love her like my mum,

To me she is and will always be my mum.

KEVIN

I'm sorry things did not work out,

Mr right is somewhere, I have no doubt,

I know it's very easy for me to say,

But don't be too sad you will be ok,

Your family and friends will help you get through,

With care and support because they love you,

Things happen for a reason, I believe in fate,

You will find Mr right because you are great,

Whoever he is, the luckiest guy he will be,

Then you will be happy, you will see.

AGA

Aga is the girl I work with she is meant

To start at eight,

She is not good at the time keeping and she always

Turns up late,

She comes into the kitchen and says 'Marco

Will you help me'.

I'm so tired and I have to make a sandwich

Lunch for three,

All she does is talk all day she can go

On and on forever,

Asking non-stop questions will they ever

Stop, no never!

Many customers lining up all wanting

Their hot drinks,

Will this queue ever end is probably

What she thinks,

After serving lunch she then goes

And has her break,

Sits down on the sofa to eat

Her pasta bake,

She then comes to the kitchen when

Her break is through,

And says who will help me I have

So much to do,

She puts all her sandwich fillings in

The little pots,

Starts to clean the fridges and the toaster,

Then she sweeps and mops,

It's near the end of the day and

She finishes at four,

Then you see her rush around and run

Out of the door.

A BETTER PLACE

It makes me feel so very glad

To put a smile on someone's face,

To do something good makes me

Feel part of the human race,

Just a little bit of thought

To show someone that you care,

You should try and do it too

Go on and see if you dare,

Just a little smile or a good

Morning to both of you,

Hold a door open for someone

Or maybe there's an errand you can do,

You don't have to spend loads of money

Just give someone a little of your time,

Maybe write a little note or poem

You don't have to make it rhyme,

Spread the love around the world

Everywhere on land and sea,

With so much care and happiness

What a better world this could be.

WEDDING VOWS

HAPPY EVER AFTER

Happy ever after we both will be,

And together forever you will see,

Promise to love you in sickness and health,

Poorer or richer whatever our wealth,

You are my life, you are my everything,

Every little thing you ask of me I'll do anything,

Very lucky am I to have found you,

Even luckier still to be loved by you too,

Right here for you I will always be,

And I'll make you happy like you make me,

For you are the most wonderful woman I know,

The love in my heart for you I will always show,

Everyone else in the world they just don't compare,

Right here is the person with whom my life I want to share.

PLEASE GET BETTER SOON

The wonderful woman I love with all my heart,

Is so poorly, seeing her like that just tears me apart,

What can I do to help her, to make her feel better?

Everything I've tried just doesn't seem to matter.

I keep her warm, tell her I love her with a kiss,

But the sparkle from her eyes has gone, it's a miss,

I care for her, cuddle her, give her my love,

But it's really no good, it's just not enough.

I'm going out of my mind, I'm frantic with worry,

To get her better again I would gladly give all of my money,

She is my love, my soulmate and also my best friend,

There is nothing I would not do for her to get her on the mend.

What's wrong with my love, who can give me the answer?

Whatever it is, please god don't let it be cancer,

We found out today that it's something called Crohn's Disease,

So now can you make her feel better really soon please!

I had no idea what it was, so I looked it up on the net,

Inflammation of the intestine and bowel was all I could get,

I read more to see what to do and how it is treated,

Sometimes it's an operation but mostly it's medicated.

I see you in pain with your belly and haemorrhoids,

You're on a drip and they're giving you steroids,

I come and visit you in hospital every single day,

To see how you are doing and hear what they say.

I miss you in the mornings, when I come home from work and bed times very much,

Our kisses, our cuddles, our "I love you's" and I long for your touch,

We were always together or somewhere very near,

I want to be with you all the time and I wish you were here.

I hope they can make you feel better again really soon,

Because you are my world and I love you all the way to the moon,

I really want you to know how much you mean to me,

And hope you're home soon and we are as happy as can be.

Whatever this may bring, all the ups and the downs,

I am right by your side I will always be around,

We will be strong and face this both together,

I will support you and I will love you forever and ever.

EVERYONE'S IN PAIN

BUT LOVE CONQUERS ALL

I cry because the pain in my heart hurts me so very much,

I am here, I hold you, I care for you, I love you with every touch,

It feels like a knife has gone through my heart and it's twisting around,

All the little things I do for you are really not enough I have found,

I look into your eyes and see you suffering in so much pain,

Your body has been through so much it is now showing all the strain,

I want so much to make you better and take all the pain away,

If I could trade places with you to do so I would do it now today,

There is nothing I would not do for you but make you better I cannot do,

But I do know for sure that I can promise this to you,

I will always be by your side and will pick you up off of the floor,

I will cherish and adore you, care for you and love you forever more.

TREASURE IS THE MEANING OF LOVE

Treasure is not a large chest full of gold,

Something shiny so still and so cold.

Treasure can be something not worth an amount of money,

But something that's filled with the love a memory.

A little doll from your dolls house you used to play with at your nans,

Mum and dad bought loads of your little brother's cars and vans.

A black leather watch with the sun and moon your uncle bought your mum,

The Father's Day poem you wrote for your dad that cost no sum.

The keyring of a train ticket that was given to you by your wife,

That has the date of your wedding and was the best day of your life.

The photographs of your family and friends in their frames,

The much-loved pets you had, and you picked out their names.

The blue jumper that was given to you by your friend,

The little blue bear you bought for someone but kept yourself in the end.

Your mind and heart, is a locked box of memories and love,

The fresh air you feel on your face and the sound of a dove.

The taste of your nans cooking you always found moreish,

The book of your life with love and emotion you cherish.

The thought you have in your head of all your hopes and dreams,

There's no greater thing in the world than love it seems.

Treasure is not a large chest full of gold,

Something shiny so still and so cold.

Treasure can be something not worth an amount of money,

But something that's filled with the love a memory.

NOT INTELLIGENT, BUT NO LESS OF A PERSON

I know I'm not intelligent, I'm not the brightest crayon in the box,

I may not be very clever, but my words could blow you off your socks.

I'm sure I am dyslexic, I was always told don't bother you won't make it,

To tell me I wasn't trying, I was stupid, I'd feel like I'd been hit.

Not everyone can be intelligent but that doesn't make you less of a person,

You must be good at something else that's probably the reason.

Maybe you have motivation and ambition to be creative,

Or work by helping other people in the care and love you give.

Maybe you make coffee's and really love to cook and bake,

I know I'm not a lawyer and lots of money I do not make.

I couldn't be a surgeon, a doctor, therapist or nurse,

But I do know I'm a good person with a heart full of love about to burst.

I may not be the sharpest tool in the box, but I am still a person too,

I do know I have the most commitment and pride in everything I do.

Please do not think less of me because you are much smarter,

I am trying to be the best person I can be, and no one could ever try harder.

It takes a lot of courage to show the real person that's inside of me,

Please don't make fun of me, look deep within and see the person I can be.

I'd love to think of myself to be some kind of poet,

Maybe deep within my heart somewhere really, I do know it.

LYN AND LOU

It will soon be time for you to go and move away,

The beginning of your lives, starts with a brand-new day.

Moving in together and making a loving home,

A new start for you both with a place all of your own.

I know it's a bit scary but it's oh so exciting too,

So many happy times together are wished for both of you.

Lots of things for you both to do that's filled with so much fun,

Now you both have each other and have found the one.

We wish you both a life of happiness, you both deserve no less,

We love you both as our friends and wish you all the best.

DEBBIE

To me she is my sister and her name is Debs,

I love it when she cuddles me she really hugs the best.

I get on very well with her she's just like my best friend,

We can talk for hours the conversation does not end.

We go and do lunch together whenever she is around,

And she also loves my own cooking too I have found.

I feel she understands me and all the thoughts I have in my head,

Sometimes she is thinking exactly what I've just said.

We are very similar in so many different ways,

She's such a good listener and I always respect what she says.

I find she's very caring and has a loving touch,

To me she is my sister and I love her very much.

CROHN'S DISEASE

My wife suffers from something called Crohn's Disease,

It is inflammation of the bowel and the intestine.

Fresh fruit and vegetables she cannot digest,

Brown bread, cereal or any fibre is not best.

She tries not to cry but you can see she's in so much pain,

Holds her tummy in her hands and rolls over again and again.

She has blood and mucus that comes out from down below,

Her legs get very sore and it makes her walking very slow.

She has haemorrhoids because she has to use the bathroom a lot,

This is such a horrible disease that she has got.

She hasn't eaten anything for almost five or six weeks,

She is so weak now she finds it hard to stand upon her feet.

She's becoming very thin, she has lost so much weight,

On so much medication, taking all her tablets, she does hate.

You can see her body is looking very frail,

Her eyes are dark, and her little face is pale.

She is so weak I have to help her bathe,

Her legs and under her arms I give a little shave.

I gently shampoo and condition her hair,

And I softly wash her body soaping everywhere.

She's had an MRI scan, and the camera up and down,

She really didn't like it, it made her wear a frown.

We have to see the specialist at Chase Farm Hospital on the twenty fifth,

And she has to have a blood test at Barnet Hospital on the sixth.

The nurse at Chase Farm on Thursday, can't do any other day at all,

So many hospital appointments the calendars getting full,

I make her a hot water bottle to help her with her tummy,

And I cook homemade soup that I try to make yummy.

I tell her I love her, and I kiss her on her head,

I hold her in my arms as we both lay in our bed.

Everything I do is just not enough though so hard I have tried,

I care for her so much and will forever be by her side.

Crohn's Disease is one of the most horrible things to ever have,

My wife is very brave and will forever have all my love.

WENDY

Wendy is a wonderful woman and she is my friend,

I can say anything to her, I don't have to pretend.

She's been through so much in her life, but she's always stayed so strong,

She's a very caring person and makes me feel like I belong.

Wendy has been there for me through all my times of woe,

When we do the quiz at darts the answers she does know.

Presentation darts nights a lot of trophies we have won,

Boogied on the dance floor having lots of fun.

I have so much respect for her she's an amazing friend to have,

She is a total inspiration and a friend I'll always love.

THEATRE

There is something about the theatre that is just so wonderful,

Everything on stage just seems to be so magical.

Small or big theatres the seats are always filled,

Happy faces on the public, they are all so very thrilled.

Everyone's participating shouting he's behind you,

When the villain comes on stage they begin to hiss and boo.

All the colourful costumes that transform all the cast,

No one ever wants it to end, time always goes so fast.

All the scenery and stage effects are all totally amazing,

The fantastic actors and actresses make it so exciting.

ALZHEIMER'S

Sitting in your chair staring up into the sky,

A lump in my throat, a tear comes in my eye.

You ask the same question for the fifteenth time today,

I tell you again and assure you everything will be ok.

I put the kettle on, make us both a cup of tea,

Give you a cuppa and a biscuit, how I wish you remembered me.

I think of the memories we made, and the happy times we've had,

Your jokes, your laugh, your smile, even the tears when we were sad.

You ask the same question for the sixteenth time today,

I give you a smile as my answer I relay.

What I wouldn't give, to hear you tell a joke again,

I'd love to hear you laugh, instead all I feel is pain.

You always looked so smart, everything was in its place,

Now your shirt is buttoned wrong and tea is dripping down your face.

You ask the same question for the seventeenth time today,

I ask god why as once again I start to pray.

I cook for you roast beef with Yorkshire pudding is your favourite,

And make you take your tablets so you don't forget to do it.

Looking through the window, I remember how you loved to do the gardening,

Now weeds are growing, and you don't even know what is happening.

You ask the same question for the eighteenth time today,

I see you sitting there but your spark has gone away.

Now you are in heaven, your soul has moved on, now you are free,

You are now who you once were, you can now remember me.

FOR THE LOVE OF KITTENS

I would love to have two little kittens,

I would name them Alfie and Oscar.

I would take such good care of them,

And I would love them forever and ever.

I don't mind what breed they would be,

I don't mind what colour I'd get.

I don't mind cleaning up after them,

They would make such a wonderful pet.

I'd let them both sit on my lap,

And I would cuddle them every day.

I'd always remember to feed them,

And I'd stroke them where ever they lay.

My mother in law lives with us at the moment,

She doesn't really like animals at all.

She's a little bit scared of them really,

And worries they might cause her to fall.

So, we can't get two little kittens yet,

But when we have a house of our own,

We'll go and get two little fluff balls,

Then we'll give Alfie and Oscar a home.

MY WEDDING DAY

My wedding day was the best day of my life,

When my true love and soulmate became my wife.

My dad was so proud to walk me down the aisle,

He looked so smart and had a huge smile.

The mums looked beautiful and had a tear in their eye,

When we said our wedding vows it made everyone cry.

We wrote our own vows, written from the heart,

Poetry has always been our thing from the start.

I always wanted to get married, it's a dream come true,

And now at last legally we both said I do.

My best man was Rich he gave a great speech,

Debbie read a poem, they both wrote one each.

Four different tiers we had on our wedding cake,

And favours with keyrings for people to take.

Luther Vandross, Here and now was our first dance,

With our arms around each other and our eyes in a trance.

Family and friends came from both near and far,

Becoming acquainted as they chat by the bar.

Busting their moves, having a boogie on the dance floor,

Laughing and joking wanting fun more and more.

The end of the night we had the honeymoon suite,

Where we shared a bath and soothed our feet.

We opened our cards and read what they said,

Before turning in and going to our four-poster bed.

We had the most wonderful day when we became wife and wife,

And now we are so happy at the start of our new life.

CANCER

A lump is found,

Heart falls to the ground.

Begins with surgery,

It's all a worry.

First no hair,

It's just not fair.

In so much pain,

Tears can't refrain.

Chemotherapy

Load so heavy.

Become so sick,

Time starts to tick.

Become so thin,

Please don't give in.

Become so pale,

Cry turns to a wail.

A battle won,

The lucky one.

A battle lost,

Heartbroken with loss.

Always so brave,

Now at peace in your grave.

Call it Cancer,

Can't find the answer?

MARCO

Marco was my boss and he's always been my mate,

He is a lovely person and I think that he is great.

He has a lot of passion in the cooking that he does,

He likes to make all different things, I think it gives him a buzz.

The food he makes and serves tastes absolutely delicious,

Most of it is good for you and is also very nutritious.

The customers love Marco's food, they always leave so happy,

He gets lots of compliments, they think his food is tasty.

He runs around the kitchen, he likes to be put to the test,

He is always so very busy, and his food is always the best.

But he also loves to party, he likes to go out for a pint,

Loves the bar in Camden, he could dance up there all night.

Marco got married to Anna, she became his wife,

She is a beautiful person and they have a happy life.

They both work very hard in the jobs that they do,

And when they're not at work they love to travel all over too.

I used to work with Marco, we worked hard but we had fun,

Marco's not my boss anymore but a good friend he has become.

We'll have to meet up soon again and go out for a pint,

Catch up on all the gossip over a couple of drinks one night.

I know we don't see each other often but we will always keep in touch,

I am so glad I met them both and are friends I love so much.

GRIEF

The pain and the emptiness that you feel inside,

Of losing a loved one when they have died.

Nobody really ever knows what to say,

Some get scared and walk the other way.

I'm sure if you said nothing but you were just there,

Would then show someone that you really care.

Give a big hug and never want to let go,

Let's them know you have love you want to show.

All you really want to do is take their pain away,

But all you can do is be there for them at the end of the day.

The thing with grief is that you are not alone,

There's lots of people that are in the same zone.

All try to be strong, to be there for each other.

And trying to make the bad situation better.

You are strong for others, but you too still have to grieve,

Don't bottle it up, let out your emotions, let them leave.

The person you love has moved on to the next life,

But your heart feels like it's been pierced with a knife.

They might not be physically there for you to see,

But spiritually by your side they will always be.

They once lived on earth and made the world a better place,

We had the pleasure of knowing them and seeing their face.

Remember the good times, all the memories that you have,

And they will live on forever in your heart and your love.

OUR FIRST WEDDING ANNIVERSARY

I am the luckiest person to have the most wonderful woman in my life,

You made me so proud and so happy the day you became my wife.

I can't believe that our first wedding anniversary is here today,

Every day is wonderful with you as my wife I have to say.

You are so many things, you are beautiful and thoughtful, you are kind and very caring,

You are generous, you are clever, you are funny, so gentle and very loving.

You make my life so happy and everything is so exciting,

Where ever we go and whatever we do you make it so amazing.

No matter what life throws at us we will get through it, we have each other,

The painful times, the bad times and the sad times we will be together.

Since we have been together we have been through so many things already,

Holding each other's hands our strength still remains to be steady.

There are so many places to go, so many first times, so much for us to do,

Married for a year now and so happy that I have the rest of my life with you.

Special times with our family and friends and lots of holidays to take,

We can have so much fun and cherish all the treasured memories that we make.

We will get aches and pains, grey hair and wrinkles and become much slower,

But you will always be my shining star, my little sweet pea flower.

I am so lucky to have the most wonderful woman as my wife,

I will love you always as we grow old together sharing our life.

SHERYL

Friends are the family we choose for ourselves,

There for each other and will always be around.

We might not see each other for a little while,

But at the end of the phone, all we have to do is dial.

She's been let down by the people supposed to care,

But never gives up even though it's just not fair.

Puts a smile on her face and tries to stay strong,

And never really letting out that anything is wrong.

She has a handsome little boy she does everything for,

Always puts him first, the best mum could do no more.

She has always had to stand upon her own two feet,

And will never ever show any kind of defeat.

She has her opinion and knows her own mind,

Is a funny, loving person who is always very kind.

Everyone who knows her is lucky to have her as a friend,

She will always be my mate until the very end.

I am very proud of her and everything she has achieved,

She has turned out to be one of the best I do believe.

LIVE LIFE

Christmas is meant to be a happy time,

But not everyone is always feeling fine.

The loved ones we've lost make us feel sad,

We remember the good times that we've all had.

We wish they were here still sharing the fun,

But they can't be anymore, it was their time to move on.

Family is where life begins, and love never ends,

Family we choose for ourselves are called friends.

I think the most amazing thing in life is love,

It's very special and something we all need to have.

I feel love we all share is a very special gift,

A life filled with love is a life that's been lived.

Try to be understanding, helpful, sharing and caring,

Be polite, respectful, funny, happy and loving.

I reat people the way you would like to be treated yourself,

Because no amount of money can buy happiness or health.

So, make as many cherished moments as you possibly can,

Because this is your life and you only get one.

BEAUTIFUL SOULS

All the beautiful souls who have moved on way up high,

I never wanted you to leave, I never wanted to say goodbye,

Every day I think of you and wish you were still here with me,

But I know you are watching over us all even though you I cannot see,

I think of all the special memories we made and all the fun we had,

And I feel so very lucky of the love we shared, it makes me feel so glad,

I cherish every moment that we all spent together on earth,

It gives me so much happiness and makes me feel so much worth,

I live my life with positivity and try to experience as much as I possibly can,

To see the world in all its glory and make other people happy is my plan,

I may not be able to see you standing here right next to me,

But in my mind and in my heart and soul you will forever be,

For no one I have loved and lost will really ever be gone,

They live within my heart as I live my life and my heartbeat carries on.

XXX

FRIENDSHIP

Friends are like flowers you pick the best,

Always there to put each other to the test,

Whenever anyone is feeling a bit down,

It's the friends job to turn over that frown,

Have lots of fun in everything that you do,

And all laugh as much as you possibly can too,

You don't need money to have a good time,

Just good company always feels divine,

You know each other well and understand one another,

And you can talk and talk whatever the hour,

Tell each other all your hopes and fears,

Be there through the smiles and all the tears,

Not afraid to say anything to each other at all,

Always there to catch you when you fall,

You laugh so much you think you might split your side,

They have a cuddle so warm and a smile so wide,

At the end of the phone ready to drop anything if you need them to,

There isn't anything that they wouldn't do for you,

Always there in all your hopes and dreams,

Right by your side through anything it seems,

A friend shares in all your troubles and strife,

But a true friend's love is always there for life.

MIRIAM

My friend Miriam could totally light up a room,

I think she could take away any sort of gloom,

Was always so generous with her hospitality,

And she had the most wonderful personality,

Trying to feed everyone with her tasty food,

Loved having a drink, putting everyone in a good mood,

When she was young she travelled the world,

Such a lovely person with a heart of gold,

Learnt so many things and was ever so clever,

Happiness was Miriam and sadness no never,

I so much loved to hear her wonderful laugh,

And cherish all the memories that I have,

Now you've moved on the world is a duller place,

And I will always miss seeing your beautiful face,

Now you are free from your aches and pains,

And your loving memory is all that remains,

The memories I have got are now all that I have,

But my friend Miriam you will forever have my love,

A HOME FULL OF LOVE

I love the feeling of walking home down my street,

I know there is my beautiful woman there ready to greet,

I walk up the path and feel warm when I see the light on,

And I go upstairs, open my arms and kiss my perfect woman,

The most loving kiss from her beautiful soft lips,

And the safe feeling I get from her warm and tender grips,

I know she loves me by the little things she does for me,

She runs me bubbles bath's and she makes me a cup of tea,

She is always thinking of me and she buys me little gifts,

Whenever I am sad she makes me happy and my mood lifts,

I love the way my hand fits in hers like two halves of a jigsaw,

And we have both become one and I'm not alone anymore,

There are not enough words for me to begin to say how happy I am,

That I have the most wonderful wife, when I met her my life began,

My heart beats so fast, I have butterflies and my knee's shake,

My heart is so full up of love and it's all hers to take,

Knowing I will grow old with her makes me smile and gives me a glow,

And there is nothing I would not do for her and my love I will always show,

I know not everyone is as lucky as me to find a love with such emotion,

A love so deep, so pure, so true that has such an everlasting devotion,

I know how extremely lucky I am to have the most wonderful wife in the world,

And I cherish every moment with her and every kiss is like finding gold,

She is my soulmate and true love, she is my one and only,

She makes my life complete, now we have each other we will never be lonely,

We both said our own wedding vows and legally said I do,

And I meant every single word and I promise I will always love you true.

GLAD OF LIFE

Oh, I'm so glad when I awake and see a brand-new day,

I get up, get ready and I'm on the bus and I'm on my way,

Off we go down the road, oh look at those beautiful daffodils,

And further on in the distance a bright sunshine just over the hills,

Oh, just look at the beautiful blossom on all of the wonderful tree's,

And all the beautifully different colours from all of the many leaves,

All the people walking with a smile upon their face,

And all the rows of cars on the road all going to some place,

All the grass is glistening from the dew upon the ground,

All the birds are singing so beautifully, oh what a lovely sound,

Look at the ducks on the water, a coot, a mallard and a drake,

All enjoying the sun while swimming about on the lake,

When I'm on my way to work this is what I am lucky enough to see,

We should all be glad for every brand-new day and see whatever will be,

Be glad you have a precious life and just do everything,

Smile and be happy and let your eyes and heart just take everything in,

There are always other people that are more worse off than you,

So, appreciate everything you have and everything you do,

Make the most of every moment and always try to give,

Because this world is wonderful, and we are lucky we can live.

BE THE SUNSHINE

If the sky is grey and dull and it makes you feel like you don't want to play,

You can't find the sunshine in the sky to make your perfect day,

Then you yourself can be the sunshine and just brighten up the way,

For everyone else in the world to have a lovely day,

RICHARD AND LAURA

Both of you are wonderful and are meant to be together,

I feel so very lucky I have the best sister and brother,

You both are very special, and you mean a lot to me,

You have so many lovely qualities and all of them I see,

Your beauty is like sunshine, it comes from within and shines right through,

You are so very kind and thoughtful in everything you both do,

I hope you know how special you are and how you brighten up everyone's day,

And I hope you know how much everyone loves you in every single way,

Life is never easy and we all have our ups and downs,

But you make everyone's day better just by being around,

You make the world a better place and make it easier to get by,

You are the sun behind the clouds, you are the rainbow in the sky,

I really do appreciate all the little things you do,

And I hope you know, how very much I love the both of you.

XXX

YOU AWOKE ME FROM MY SLEEP

I was cold and empty until I met you,

Then you lit my fire and awoke me,

Now my lovely warm flames are glowing,

And all the different colours you can see.

My flames they move like a little dance,

Life has begun and wants to stay alive,

Fire should burn and turn into cinders,

My glow won't stop it just tries to strive.

Your vision saw something with potential,

I was so still and so alone until you saw me,

You could see that there could be beauty,

And you clearly could see what I could be.

I was cold and empty until I met you,

Then you lit my fire and awoke me,

Now my lovely warm flames are glowing,

And the colours are there for all to see.

AMAZING

It's amazing when you think about what you've been through in your life,

All the sadness and the heartache and the troubles and the strife,

You never think it will happen and you have no idea how you will pull through,

But you have to stay strong and try your best to carry on is what you do,

If only people knew they would wonder how you have managed to survive,

But you are so much stronger than you think, and you carry on and you strive,

Everyone goes through bad times, ups and downs that is just life,

All the sadness and the heartache, feels like your hearts been pierced with a knife,

But you have to remember there is always someone else worse off than you,

That they are having their own problems that they are trying to get through,

No matter what has happened you are still here to live another day,

You must carry on with life and the bad times will pass away,

We all have our bad days, feel low and cry a lot of tears,

But make the most of your life as you are lucky to live for all those years,

There might be clouds in the sky now, but a rainbow will come shining through,

So even though it's not easy, try to stay positive in everything you do,

Try your best to keep smiling and live your life to the fullest that you can,

Have as much fun as possible and try to laugh a lot is a good plan,

Remember how lucky you are and appreciate everyone and everything that you have,

Do the right thing, be there for other people and let your heart share all its love.

HERE ARE SOME POEMS WRITTEN BY MY WIFE.

WRITTEN BY SHARON DE-FREITAS

CONTENTS:

EBONY BAY

Oh, how I long to be in Ebony Bay,

And listen to what the ocean has to say.

To sit on the rocks, on the edge of the shore,

And stare into space until time is no more.

Alone with my thoughts, alone with my spirit,

The beat of my heart so loud I can hear it.

I can feel my breath, but it's caught by the breeze,

And taken to places I'll never see.

The sun is now sinking and the shoreline's ablaze,

With colours, so vivid my mind is a daze.

The beauty of nature here for all to see,

But this a private show only for me.

FOR KELLY

You took away our friendship, replaced it with something new,

I don't know where I stand anymore, I just know it's not beside you.

You only call now when you need me, never just to say hello,

And if I try to talk some more you say you have to go.

I feel as if I'm imposing and taking up your time,

Once a constant companion, now I'm way down on your line.

You took away our friendship, and I'm left here all alone,

One day you may know how it feels just to sit there by the phone.

You used to tell me everything, now I'm the last to know,

I was your confidant but that seems so long ago.

You took away our friendship, without even saying why,

It seems I've served my purpose, all that's left now is goodbye.

MY EVERYTHING

You are the notes of symphony

And the music of my life,

You're the leaves on the trees

You're the sugar and the spice.

You are the life that makes me live

And the dream that soothes my sleep,

You have the touch that makes me feel

You are the words that form my speech.

You are the flame that keeps me burning

And the wind beneath my wings,

You're all of this and so much more

You are my everything.

UNSAID

Ask me anything you want

And I will answer true,

But the one thing left unsaid

Is yes, I do love you.

We talk of many things

Of life and loves gone by,

But the one thing left unsaid

Is yes, for you I'd die.

Ask me anything you want

I will answer with free will,

But the one thing left unsaid

Is yes, I love you still.

NEVER

Never doubt, never worry,

For I am always there,

Never question, never cry,

Not even a single tear.

Never hurt, never leave,

I will always need your touch,

Never think I don't love you,

You will NEVER know how much.

THE COLOURS OF LOVE

Blue for loss,

And red for heat.

Yellow for fun,

And black for a cheat.

White for innocence,

And purple for lust.

Green for strength,

And gold you can trust.

ASHES

I stare into the fire-

Just sit and watch the flames-

As they dance and spit out cinders,

And I recall the names.

The names of those that I have loved-

Who showed me nothing in return-

The fire leaps as did my heart,

But now the memories I burn.

I shall burn away the sadness-

Until only ashes remain-

No remorse and no regret,

There can be no one to blame.

ONLY WORDS

My day are letters

That I form into words,

These words shape my thoughts

But are seldom heard.

I string them along

Until a verse I have found,

And soon there's a poem

Of my life with no sound.

But these are only words

Trying to make my life rhyme,

To know me takes longer

Can you spare the time?

THE LITTLE THINGS

A breath of fresh air,

Just one drop of rain.

A ray of sunshine,

A mountain terrain.

The first light of morning,

A cool glass of water.

Songs full of memories,

An old woman's laughter.

A kiss without warning,

The changing of season.

One look from your eyes,

A hug for no reason.

UNFULFILLED

I am a book with no words and a song without a tune,

I am an empty bottle and a star without a moon,

I am a driver with no car and a painter with no muse,

A believer with no faith and a thinker who's confused.

SORRY

The door slams and voices rise,

Tempers flare and someone cries,

Things are said and their meaning,

Cause much pain and ill feeling,

No one wants to be the first,

To say sorry, and what's worse,

Is that pride gets in the way,

When all it needs is to say,

Please forgive me I was wrong,

But the battles carry on.

MY WISHES FOR YOU

I wish you happiness and joy,

A strength of heart and mind,

A love that fills your world,

And makes your eyes blind.

I wish you all these things,

That I've never had myself,

So, that you can tell of them,

And I can share your wealth.

AFTER

After the storm the rainbow,

After the night, the dawn,

After I knew I loved you,

Only then was my heart re-born.

After the final kisses,

After the wave goodbye,

After I knew you'd left me,

Only then did I want to die.

After the longing left me,

After the time slipped by,

After the new storm rages,

Only then will I cease to cry.

AFTER YOU

Huddled in the corner – hiding from the storm,

Rain lashing the window – trying hard to stay warm,

Lightening pierced the darkness – lit up the room like day,

No one here to comfort me – now you have gone away,

The thunder crashes down – And I scream out in pain,

The hurt is in my heart – My tears are all in vain,

The earth now has your body – and heaven has your soul,

All I have are memories – to keep me from the cold,

Whenever I hear thunder – and storm clouds fill the sky,

I huddle in the corner – and think of life gone by.

AS IF BY MAGIC

She appeared as if by magic, this angel of the road

She offered conversation, and to share my heavy load

No more wandering in darkness, with a hand to lead the way

Now a light is in the distance, and a meaning to the day.

She appeared as if by magic, this harbinger of fear

She whispered words of wisdom, but so soft I couldn't hear

No more surety of action, second guessing all the time

Planted doubts of my sub-conscious, till my words no longer rhyme.

She was gone the next morning, but her imprint on the sheet

Left memories so powerful, I could still feel her heat

Sometimes when I'm sleeping, I think I hear her call

And then as if by magic, I remember it all.

KISS OF LOVE

Your hand on my face,

Then your lips touch mine,

So gentle and loving,

The feelings divine,

Your tongue starts to venture,

I'm lost in your kiss,

So deep and so hungry,

This feeling is bliss.

OUTSIDE THE TOUCH OF TIME

A sister is a little bit of childhood that can never be lost,

To the outside world, we may look like we grow older and wiser,

Our hair may be greying and our reflexes slower,

But we know each other as we always were, we know each other's hearts,

We live outside the touch of time.

With pictures that are worth a million words,

I look through old photos watching memories made over a lifetime,

Through the years, we have seen many things,

Travelled many miles, ebbing and flowing like the tide,

Our lives so different yet still collide.

As your wedding day arrives,

And there you stand so different yet still the same,

I'm sure no one would disagree, on how beautiful you look,

And how full your heart is of love,

I wish you and Gary all the love in the world.

Thank you for all the memories that I hold so close to my heart,

And for all the new memories to come,

Life may try and change us and place obstacles in our way,

But we know each other as we always were, we know each other's hearts,

We live outside the touch of time.

ONE DAY

One day at a time one kiss at a time, that's all I have to give

One love at a time one life at a time, that's all I have to live,

I give you my days I give you my kisses, I give you my life and my love,

I hope you accept my offerings sent on the wings of a dove.

WORDS FLOW

Words flow between us, back and forth like the tide,

Days come, and days go, and we sail along for the ride,

No stormy weather here, all is calm all is serene,

The view goes on forever, we both wonder is this a dream,

Up ahead in the distance a glimmering light so bright,

It may take a while to get there but we sail on through the night.

PHOENIX

Come to me in a whisper,

Come on the wings of a storm,

Come and feel my passion,

We'll make love until dawn.

Come to me in a heartbeat,

Come in the flame of desire,

Come and take the chance,

Be reborn in the fire.

HAM AND CHEESE

Ham and cheese, I love you so,

With or without mayo,

In some bread or a baguette,

Nothing I've found can beat you yet,

Honey roast and English cheddar,

The taste of you there is none better.

NIC LEMON

Never knew such feelings,

I didn't think I ever would,

Can't believe it's happening,

Love has never felt so good,

Every day is an adventure,

My heart and mind begin to race,

Only you can make me feel this,

Now I'm longing for your taste.

FEELINGS

There are times in my life when I felt so alone,

No place in this world that I could call home.

The future was blurred with nothing to see,

I accepted that this was the way it would be.

Something so wrong with me deep inside,

Days came and went as I ebbed with the tide.

Planning for nothing and hoping for less,

Feelings all locked up, emotions a mess.

Then into my life without any warning,

An angel appeared a new life was dawning.

Forgotten feelings now rise to the top,

Rushing through me may they never stop.

I WANT TO GROW OLD WITH YOU

I want to grow old with you, forget things and learn them anew.

I want to stare into your eyes, each day with wonder and surprise.

I want to hold your hand and smile, walking together mile after mile.

I want to hear all your hopes and fears, even if it takes a million years.

I want to hold you while you cry, and love you till the day I die.

I want to grow old with you, forget things and learn them anew.

BEFORE YOU

Before you the days went on forever,

Every hour and minute dragged on,

Fading memories of love and laughter,

Only heard and recalled in a song.

Right now my heart is bursting,

Every fibre aches for your touch.

You and I will soon be together,

Only you know this means so much.

Until Sunday my love xxx.

LIFE IS A DANCE

Life is a dance,

It takes time to learn the steps.

We may not always follow the rhythm,

And sometimes the tune is unfamiliar,

But we listen, and we learn.

Can I have this dance with you?

COME WITH ME

I want you to come with me

As many times as we dare

Ignoring even the daybreak

Making love without a care.

I want you to come with me

As I kiss slowly down your spine

Exploring every inch of you

Just because you are mine.

I want you to come with me

As our passion starts to rise

To hear you call out my name

As I look in your eyes.

JUST THE THOUGHT

Just the thought of you can do it

Or when I look in your eyes.

Just knowing that you love me

Is a constant surprise.

Realising how much I love you

And knowing I always will.

Realising that we are forever

All my days and nights you fill.

I wonder how I managed

Without you in my life.

I filled my days with nothing

One day you will be my wife.

Now that I have found you

Just watch us as we fly.

Now that we have each other

Our love will never die.

SOLITAIRE

At first, I hardly noticed

The tear falling down my face,

But one tear turned to many

And my mind began to race.

If I am being honest

And to myself I must be true,

I know why I was crying

For a love I never knew.

I see it all around me

People travelling in pairs,

But I am always lonely

All the happiness is theirs.

Will it ever happen to me?

Will I find someone to share,

All this love I have within

Or will I play solitaire?

YOU

You are my soul, you are my life

You are my day and night.

You are the smile that brightens up my world,

You are my one true ray of light.

Without you I would be alone,

Without you I would die.

Without you nothing would make sense

Without you I wouldn't even try.

Now that I have you, I make plans

Now that I know you care.

Now that my dreams can all come true

Now that the future I can bare.

One day I know we will be one,

One day our lives can start.

One day I'll take you as my wife,

One day we'll never be apart.

The little things you do for me,

The way you make me feel,

The touch of your warm hand in mine,

The knowledge that this is real.

I offer you my deepest love,

I offer all that you see.

I offer you everything I am,

I offer you all that I will be.

There is nothing I wouldn't do for you,

There is nowhere I wouldn't go.

There is nothing that I would ever hide,

There is nothing I wouldn't show.

So many firsts are still to come,

So many memories to make.

So many lives for us to live,

So many journeys to take.

You are my soul, you are my life,

You are my day and night.

You are the meaning in my world,

You are what makes things right.

GORGEOUS

Gorgeous is what you are to me,

Others may have failed to see.

Right before their very eyes,

Given away I don't know why.

Every day I thank the stars,

Once their mistake but never ours.

Under the sky there is no other,

Sensational, wonderful as my lover.

SEASONS OF LOVE

The mornings now are darker

As if even the sun doesn't want to rise.

What hope is there for the worker,

Without the sun to prise open their eyes?

The days now all seem longer,

From dawn till dusk we toil,

We dream and reflect on the summer,

That autumn has come to spoil.

Yet even in the darkness,

I constantly dream of you still.

The warm touch of your caress,

That's how my days I fill.

For you my love are my warmth and sun,

You are my long joyous days.

Even when autumn has come and gone,

And winter brings the next phase.

Of all the seasons, none can compare,

With the smile from my baby's lips.

Even the summer as hard as it dares,

For in my heart and mind, she sits.

So, roll on winter, roll on spring,

Each day will be the same.

Only my lover can make me sing

And burst my heart with flames.

MISSING YOU

I count the days each time we meet,

Until I will see you again.

The days are long, but the nights are sweet,

Until I will see you again.

I count the hours since we last spoke,

Until I hear you again.

I remember you laughing at my joke,

Until I hear you again.

I count the minutes since I've seen your smile,

Until I will see you again.

I count the seconds since we last kissed,

Until I can touch you again.

Each embrace, that we've lost and missed,

Until I can touch you again.

I count the years we will be together,

And I will never let you go.

I know these years will go on forever,

And I will never let you go.

I WAS IN THE DARKNESS

I was in the darkness,

So, darkness I became.

Then in the distance I saw a light,

And strained to hear its name.

I could not believe that you were there,

Somewhere waiting for me.

My heart had hoped for a love like yours,

But my eyes they could not see.

I wish I'd known you sooner,

To save the heartache and tears.

Although it took so long to find you,

They were not wasted years.

My life has made me who I am,

And led me to your door.

So now I can deserve your heart,

And be yours for evermore.

MY VALENTINE

If kisses were raindrops, I'd send you showers.

If hugs were seconds, I'd give you hours.

If smiles were water, I'd send you the sea.

If love was a person, I'd send you me.

WEDDING VOWS

I offer you my deepest love,

I offer all that you see.

I offer you everything I am,

I offer you all that I will be

I want to grow old with you, forget things and learn them anew.

I want to stare into your eyes, each day with wonder and surprise.

I want to hold your hand and smile, walking together mile after mile.

I want to hear all your hopes and fears, even if it takes a million years.

I want to hold you while you cry, and love you till the day I die.

I want to grow old with you, forget things and learn them anew.

You are my soul, you are my life,

You are my day and night,

You are the meaning in my world,

You are what makes things right.

MY LOVE FOR YOU

My love for you is deeper now, a

Year has passed, I don't know how.

Like yesterday, it seems to me,

Our vows were said, I became we.

Valentine's day comes all the time,

Every day that you are mine.

Forever and always, I love you so,

Our love can only continue to grow.

Right by your side through good and bad.

Your loves the best I've ever had.

One year will turn into eternity.

Until the end of time, it's you and me.

XXX

ACKNOWLEDGEMENTS

I would like to thank my wife, Sharon, my Mum and Dad and all my family and friends for making me the person I am today and making all the special moments in my life and my book.

We all go through so many things in life, the ups and the downs, and it really makes me appreciate everyone I have and love in my life.

I love all my family and friends with all my heart. You all mean the world to me, you are my world. You all make the world a better place just by being in it.

I hope you all enjoyed my book you all have helped me to make it what it is.

Thank you,

Love always Nic xx